for C.B.
~Elisabeth Brami

Library of Congress Cataloging-in-Publication Data available upon request.

First published in English copyright © 1996 Abbeville Press.

ISBN 0-7892-0046-5

First edition
1 2 3 4 5 6 7 8 9 10

Little pleasures

Elisabeth Brami
Philippe Bertrand

Abbeville Press Publishers
New York London Paris

The smell of toast and coffee while you are getting up.

Having a funny

face contest with

yourself in the mirror.

Starting a

collection of anything-

it doesn't matter what.

Breathing in freshly
cut grass, then
taking a fistful of it
and smelling it
with your eyes closed.

Finding a full

jar of jam

in your cupboard.

Not stepping

on

the cracks

in the sidewalk.

Quietly

watching a fly

walk ⚡ around

on your stomach

and tickle you.

Smelling the savory
chickens roasting in
the deli as you stroll by.

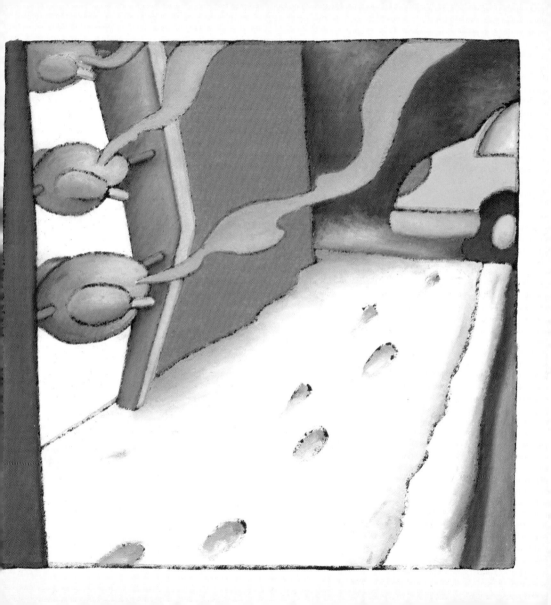

Covering

your ears

and pretending

the world

is always this quiet!

A bowl to lick,

especially one

a chocolate cake

was mixed in.

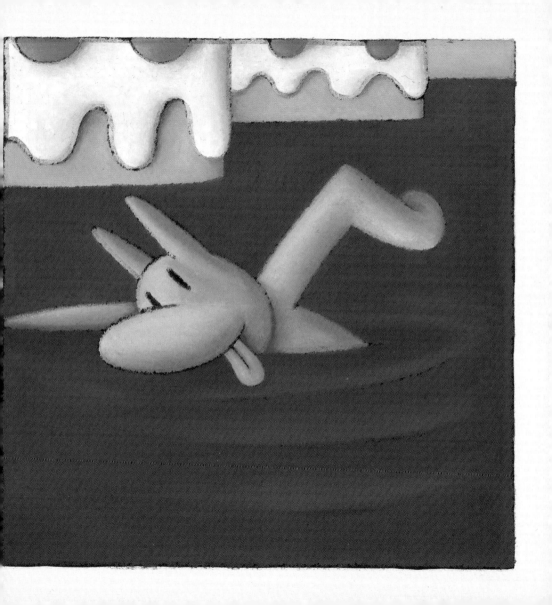

Doodling.

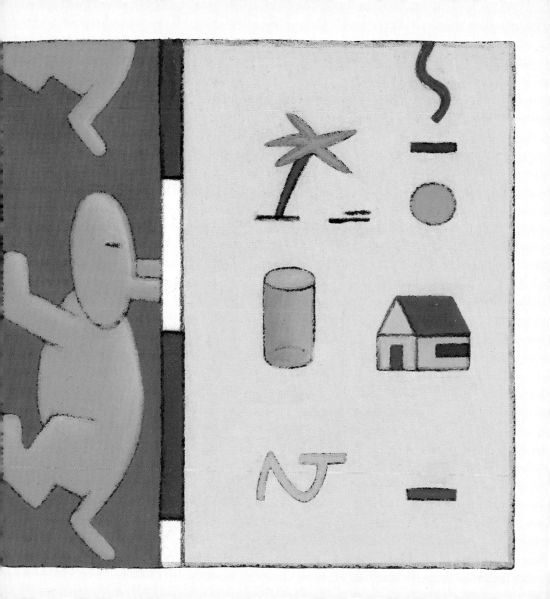

 Scratching

yourself where it

really itches.

Swearing under
your breath.

Waiting (in the quiet
of a warm summer night
for a shooting star
to wish upon.

Finding

mysterious shapes

in the shadows

and cracks

on the wall.

Counting the
red cars you see
on a long trip.

Running an ice-cube

all over your face

when you are

hot and sweaty.

Inventing

words and phrases

in a language

that only you know.

Hanging cherries

over your ears.

Watching the clouds change shape as they drift by, like magical creatures in a cartoon.

Smelling the

inviting scent

of a new book.

Making it

to the bathroom

when you've really

got to go.

Shuffling through

piles of leaves

and hearing

them crackle.

The company of all

your stuffed animals

when you go to sleep.

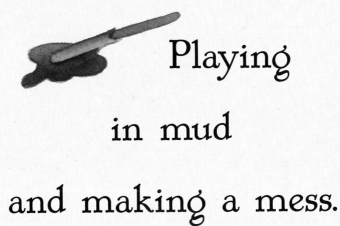

Playing

in mud

and making a mess.

Keeping

gumballs

around your house.

Breaking off and eating a piece of fresh, crusty bread before you even leave the bakery.

Staying home

and

pampering yourself

when

you're ![bottle] sick.

Finding a cool part
of the sheet
when the bed
feels too hot.

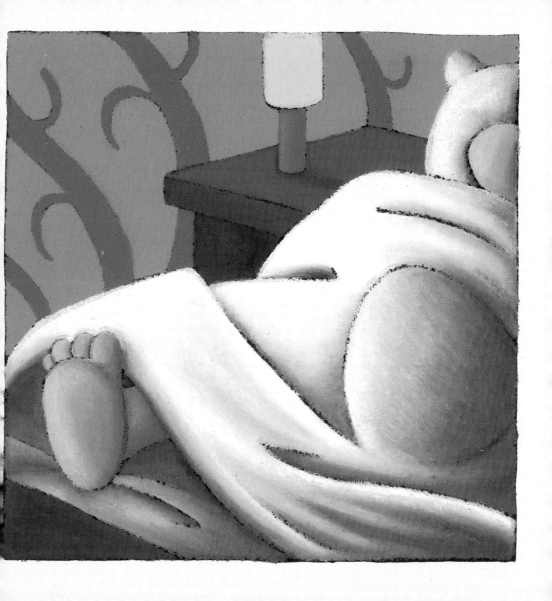

Looking for

flying saucers

in the night sky.

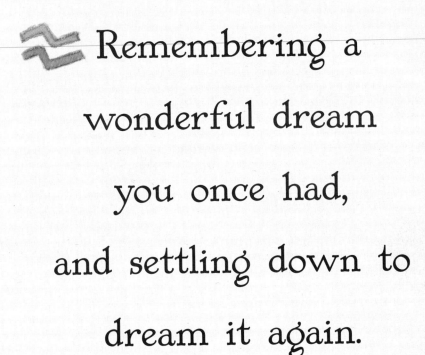 Remembering a wonderful dream you once had, and settling down to dream it again.

Reading Peter Pan

and believing

that you can   fly.

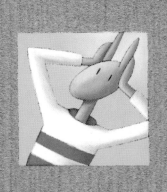